To: _____

From: _____

Date: _____

Ciana Publishers is dedicated to changing lives through books. Children will be empowered through the "What Would Jesus Do Series". Through these books, we spread the Good News of Jesus Christ, the hope of glory.

– SJvR & LS

Copyright © 2022 by Sybrand JvR & Lucia S.
All rights reserved. Published by Ciana Publishers

This Book is Copyright Protected:
This is only for personal use. You cannot amend, distribute, sell, use, quote, or paraphrase any part of the content within this book without the consent of the author. The Author guarantees all contents are original and do not infringe upon the legal rights of any other person or work.

No part of this book may be reproduced, duplicated, or transmitted in any form by means such as printing, scanning, photocopying, or otherwise, without direct written permission from the author or publisher, except for the use of quotations in a book review and as permitted by the U.S. copyright law.
For permission, contact info@cianapublishers.com.

Disclaimer and Terms of Use:
This book is provided solely for entertainment, motivational and informational purposes.

All Scripture quotations, unless otherwise indicated, are taken from the Holy Bible, New International Version®, NIV®. Copyright ©1973, 1978, 1984, 2011 by Biblica, Inc.TM Used by permission of Zondervan. All rights reserved worldwide. www.zondervan.comThe "NIV" and "New International Version" are trademarks registered in the United States Patent and Trademark Office by Biblica, Inc.TM

Authors – Sybrand JvR & Lucia S

3rd Edition 2024

www.cianapublishers.com

CHARACTER DESCRIPTIONS

Ji-hoon

Ji-hoon mostly dwells in his own world, being a perfectionist
and introverted genius who is exceptionally loyal.
He loves playing chess, and his dream is to become a great mathematician.
He is well-read and speaks with wisdom.
He is calm, calculated, and very protective and acts like Elsa's big brother.
He loves Jesus a lot and this love overflows to others.

Elsa

Elsa is a bubbly, self-assured go-getter who isn't afraid to speak
her mind and she is quick to act. Her strengths are that she is bold,
confident, and fearless. She loves to dance, play drums,
and play sports. She is always looking for adventure.
As a spontaneous ball of happiness, when she's around,
excitement is sure to follow. Her favourite Bible character is
Esther, who made a big difference in her surroundings.

Ruby

Ruby is from a well-to-do family and is like a little princess.
She is spoiled and loves shopping and dancing.
She is smart and witty and a take-no-nonsense kind of girl.
It does take her a while to warm up to new friends.
But once she becomes your friend, she is loyal and kind.

Pete

Pete is a disciplined and dedicated swimmer.
His dream is to take part in the Olympics.
His challenges have taught him to be a fighter.
He has a good heart and enjoys making people laugh.
He likes to test how far he can push the limits with a bit of mischief.

Mrs Harris

Mrs Harris has a kind heart and a listening ear. She gives good advice.
She is pretty strict and demands good discipline and
respect for each other. Mrs Harris is very caring,
and is always ready to go the extra mile.

HAVE YOU EVER... DID YOU EVER...

Have you ever been so mad you wanted to
yell at the top of your lungs?

Did you ever stay mad at someone
for a really, really long time?

Have you ever goofed up and felt
super sorry afterwards?

What's your go-to move when you realise
you've made a mistake?

Guess what? Ji-hoon and Elsa had no clue what
their day was going to be like!

If only we know how much we need Jesus. We need Him
in every area of our lives.

Wanna see how Ji-hoon and Elsa got through their
wild roller coaster day?

Let's dive in and find out!

 I can't believe that the summer holiday is over. I wish I could have a few more days. Still, I can't wait to see my friends.

 Did you know we are getting a new maths teacher, Mrs Harris? She has a master's degree in maths and was first in her class. I can't wait to pick her brain.

 Maths, oh, please! SERIOUSLY!!! Are there any other ten-year-olds who are SO excited about maths and teachers?

 You know that maths is the foundation of everything? Right?

 There is only one Ji-hoon; you missed school way too much.

 Can't you open your eyes?

 Even if I have four eyes, you shouldn't walk into the road, period.

 You don't even say sorry. What is wrong with you?

 Why should I apologise? You can't even stay on the pavement with two eyes. I don't have time for this, and by the way, you seem to be doing just fine.

 Are you okay? Are you hurt?

 I'm fine. Miss New Girl in Town has some attitude. I'm ready to show her how things work in THIS town.

 You know how you become when you get angry. I am not going to bandage you up again.

 Prepare your bandages for the New Girl in Town.

 You have to calm down. Let's count to ten. One... two...

 One two, Elsa's coming for you!

 I was hoping for a lovely day, but storms are brewing on the horizon.

 Not the horizon; they're right HERE!

 Look! There is Miss New Girl in Town's bike.

 Settle down, Elsa.

 Settle down…! My BACKSIDE is still sore!

 Aren't you looking forward to seeing your friends? Come on, let's go and greet them.

 Why are you standing so close to my bike?

 I'm looking for you.

 Well, here I am!… So?

 There's the new maths teacher. Come on, Elsa, let's go!

 This is why I am looking for you.
LOOK OUT! Miss New Girl in Town.

 OUCH!!!

 Ooh, did that hurt?
You can be glad your eyes can still see.

 If your eyeballs are still in their sockets at the end of this day, then I'm not yours, TRULY, Miss Ruby.

 PLEASE!

You two sort yourselves out.
Mrs Harris! Mrs Harris! Good morning Ma'am!

 Can someone EXPLAIN what is going on here?

 She hit me with her bag!

 She hit me with her bike!

 She walked into the road!

 And you, mister, hmm…?

 It was an accident. I was very excited to meet you and show you the formulas I worked on.

 Couldn't you have stopped the fight?

 Ma'am, they are both stubborn. It is their way or the highway. I prefer not to get crushed between two trucks.

 All of you! Go and wait outside the principal's office. Now!

 Girls, you heard the principal. No extra mural activities after school. You have to sort out the recycling.

 It wasn't my fault.

 Well, it wasn't mine.

 That's enough. Get back to your class. And Ji-hoon, next time, you need to be more careful.

 Yes, Ma'am.

 I have no doubt that you two will soon learn to work together.

 Maybe if she puts a STOP SIGN on her back, she won't get knocked over.

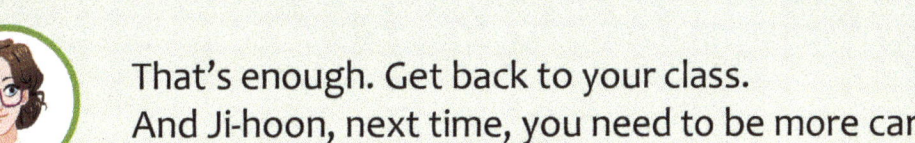 Ruby! That is uncalled for.

 You're to blame for this!

 What? You spoiled my first day. Don't stand so close to me!

 You should go for cycling lessons.

 You should recycle your mouth.

 Yo! Ladies. Pete's finally back in the house! How is everyone doing?

 What's going on here?
I see some lightning. Are you girls fighting?

 Mind your own business.

 Move aside, ladies, and listen to Uncle Pete's jokes.

 Oh boy, what kind of school did my mum put me in?

 Knock, knock. Who's there? Trash. Trash who? 'Trash-ladies'.

 Goodness! Is this for real?

 Oh please! This is what you call a joke without a punchline.

 Do your parents even know you are here?

 Well, I know where they are, but they don't know where I am.

 Oh, I get it. You are supposed to be at a different school.
Clearly, you don't listen to your parents.
See where you are on the first day of school.

 Well, at least I'm not alone. This says a lot about you guys.

 Elsa, who is this girl with the attitude?

 I'm yours Truly, Miss Ruby.

 Oh please!

 Well, catch this trash, Miss TT, aka Truly Trash.

 No! What are you doing?

Ha-ha-ha!!!

 No! You'll get us into trouble.

 Pete, STOP! I'm going to call Mrs Harris.

 No! I will call her RIGHT NOW!

 Yeah, right. Go ahead; I don't care.

Now I'm fed up. I'm going!

Really, Pete! Elsa, I'm joining you.

 Sorry, sorry! I will stop.

 Why do you need to be threatened before you stop?

 Why, Pete? Is it for attention?

 Don't you get attention at home, really?

 No! I don't have parents. Are you happy now?

 Sorry, Pete, we did take it a bit far.

 Yes, I feel so bad for mentioning your parents. Please forgive me.

 No worries. You didn't know.
I am sorry for calling you 'Trash-ladies'.

 That's okay. You did catch us doing the trash for something trashy we did.

 Shouldn't there be a few more 'sorries'?...

 Ruby, I'm sorry that I got so angry.

 I'm also sorry for being so rude.

 Let's get together this weekend for a swim at my house.

 Oh wow, that will be amazing!

 COOL! Swimming is my thing. Knock, knock.

 Who's there?

 It's so cool to have you as my new friend.

 We are one another's strength.
Come here, Yours Truly, Miss Ruby, and give me a BIG HUG.

 Hi, Ji-hoon. You're still around?
Let me introduce my new friend, Ruby.

 Hi, Ji-hoon.

 Nice to meet you, Ruby.
I've been helping Mrs Harris set up her class.
I also showed her some of my maths formulas.

 And we had help solving our friendship formula.

 I knew the two of you could formulate your friendship. I can't wait to hear all about it.

 Well, it all started with 'Trash-ladies'.

  Ha! Ha! Ha!

WHAT WOULD JESUS DO?

 Ji-hoon, today was like a wild roller coaster ride. I messed up big time. But in the end, Ruby and I said sorry and became friends. She's really cool. I like her.

 I'm proud of you, Elsa. Your escapades remind me of a story about Peter and Jesus.

 Which story? There are so many, aren't there?

 Well, there's this one night when Jesus was taken away by some mean people, and it scared all of Jesus' friends. Peter followed to see what would happen but pretended he didn't know Jesus. When others asked him if he knew Jesus, then not just once, but three times he denied knowing Jesus. Then Jesus looked at Peter, and Peter felt so sad and ran away crying.

 So, Peter made a big mistake?

Illustrated by Kseniia Pavska

 Yep, a huge one. But then, Peter said sorry and became one of Jesus' best friends. Jesus wasn't mad at him. He forgave Peter because He knew what was truly inside Peter's heart.

 So, what should we learn from this?

 It shows us that everyone makes mistakes, but how we fix them is what really matters. Jesus teaches us to forgive people when they do something wrong, just like how you and Ruby became friends.

 If I had said sorry sooner, we wouldn't have spent all day being upset and being punished.

That is so true, Elsa. No one is perfect. Let us be quick to say sorry, quick to forgive, learn from our mistakes and move on.

LET'S PRAY

Father, may Your Spirit who dwells in my heart
be the voice of my prayer, in Jesus' name.

Help me to respond as You would when I am hurt.

Help me to forgive others as You forgive me.

In Jesus' name.

Amen.

BIBLE VERSES TO CHECK OUT

Ephesians 4:32, Colossians 3:13, Luke 6:37,

Luke 22:54-62, John 21:15-17, 20-22

INSPIRATIONAL QUOTES

Before you react, pause and ask yourself, "What role have I played?"

Proverbs 25:28, Haggai 1:5-7, Matthew 7:3, Luke 15:17-24

You can make a bigger mistake by reacting
badly to someone else's wrongdoing.

Genesis 50:18-21, Proverbs 15:1, Ecclesiastes 10:4, Matthew 5:38-48, Galatians 6:1

You can choose to have a bad temper or decide to be friendly.

Genesis 4:7, Proverbs 29:11, Ecclesiastes 7:9, Ephesians 4:26-27

What sweater are you wearing;
the sweater of anger or the sweater of kindness?

Psalm 37:8, Proverbs 14:29, Luke 6:27, Ephesians 4:26,31-32, James 1:19

When facing challenges, you can choose to blame someone else or choose
to see it as a learning experience and an opportunity to grow.

Genesis 50:18-21, Romans 5:3-4, James 1:2-4

LET'S CHAT

What lessons have you learned?
_____
_____
_____

What should Ruby have done differently?
_____
_____
_____

Was Elsa right to hit Ruby? How could Elsa have handled the situation differently?
_____
_____
_____

Why do you think forgiveness and showing kindness are important?
_____
_____
_____

Have you ever had a similar experience of making up with someone after a disagreement?
_____
_____
_____

What can you say about the following? "Everyone makes mistakes; Mistakes are Correctable."
_____
_____
_____

OTHER BOOKS IN
THE WHAT WOULD JESUS DO SERIES

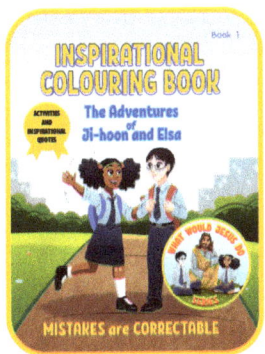    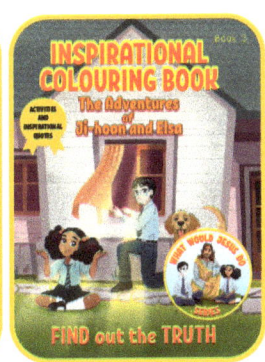

OTHER BOOKS BY THE AUTHORS

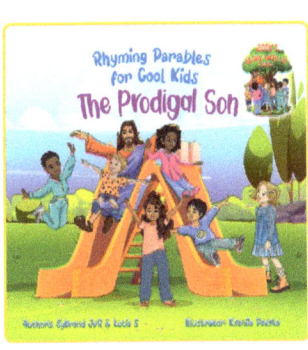   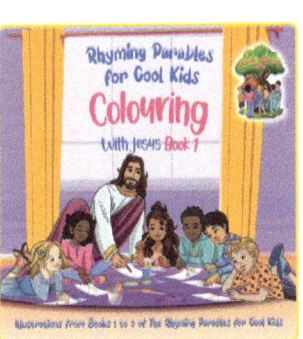

www.ingramcontent.com/pod-product-compliance
Lightning Source LLC
Chambersburg PA
CBHW061146010526
44118CB00026B/2891